W9-ATY-617

ROUND LAKE AREA
LIBRARY
906 HART ROAD
ROUND LAKE, IL 60073
(847) 546-7060

DEMCO

DK READERS

Level 4

A Note to Parents

DK READERS is a compelling program for beginning readers, designed in conjunction with leading literacy experts.

Beautiful illustrations and superb full-color photographs combine with engaging, easy-to-read stories to offer a fresh approach to each subject in the series. Each DK READER is guaranteed to capture a child's interest while developing his or her reading skills, general knowledge, and love of reading.

The four levels of DK READERS are aimed at different reading abilities, enabling you to choose the books that are exactly right for your child:

Level 1 – Beginning to read
Level 2 – Beginning to read alone
Level 3 – Reading alone
Level 4 – Proficient readers

The "normal" age at which a child begins to read can be anywhere from three to eight years old, so these levels are only a general guideline.

No matter which level you select, you can be sure that you are helping your child learn to read, then read to learn!

LONDON, NEW YORK, DELHI,
MUNICH, AND MELBOURNE

Created by Tall Tree Ltd
Editor Jon Richards
Designer Ed Simkins

For DK
Series Editor Alastair Dougall
Series Designer Rob Perry
Production Nicola Torode
Picture Researcher Harriet Mills
Picture Library Sarah Mills
Cover art by James Calafiore and
Peter Palmiotti

First American Edition, 2004

Published in the United States by
DK Publishing, Inc.
375 Hudson Street
New York, New York 10014

04 05 06 07 08 10 9 8 7 6 5 4 3 2 1

Page design copyright © 2004 Dorling Kindersley Limited

AQUAMAN, JLA, and all related characters, names, and elements
are trademarks of DC Comics © 2004. All rights reserved.

All rights reserved under International and Pan-American Copyright
Conventions. No part of this publication may be reproduced, stored
in a retrieval system, or transmitted in any form or by any means,
electronic, mechanical, photocopying, recording or otherwise,
without the prior written permission of the copyright owner.
Published in Great Britain by Dorling Kindersley Limited.

A Catalog record for this book
is available from the Library of Congress.

ISBN 0-7566-0230-0

Color reproduction by Media Development and Printing Ltd, UK
Printed and bound in China by L Rex Printing Co., Ltd.

The publisher would like to thank the following for their kind permission
to reproduce their pictures:

(Key: a=above; c=center; b=below; l=left; r=right; t=top)

7 Dorling Kindersley: National Geophysical Data Centre; 9 Seapics.com:
Doug Perrine b; 14 Bridgeman Art Library, London/New York: Christie's
Images: Katsushika Hokusai bl; 15 Corbis: Rick Doyle b; 33 Mary Evans
Picture Library: ca; 38 Nature Picture Library Ltd: Staffan Widstrand tl; 41
Image Quest Marine: Peter Herring b; 46-47 Corbis: Gustavo Gilabert c.

All other images © Dorling Kindersley. For further information, see
www.dkimages.com

Dorling Kindersley would like to thank the following artists for their
contribution to this book: Eric Battle, Ken Branch, James Calafiore,
Saleem Crawford, John Dell, Marty Egeland, Steve Epting, Ron Garney,
Drew Geraci, Tom Grindberg, Yvel Guichet, Scott Hanna,
Doug Hazlewood, Don Hillsman, Phil Jimenez, Michael Kaluta,
Scott Kolins, Doug Mahnke, José Marzan, Mike Mayhew,
Mark McKenna, Mike Miller, Tom Nguyen, Graham Nolan,
Peter Palmiotti, Joe Phillips, Howard Porter, Mark Propst, Howard Purcell,
Pablo Raimondi, Norm Rapmund, Roger Robinson, Jasen Rodriguez,
Prentis Rollins, P. Craig Russell, Paul Ryan, Steve Scott, Val Semeiks,
Howard Shum, Andy Smith, Claude St. Aubin, John Stokes,
and John Totleben.

Dorling Kindersley would also like to thank: Peter Tomasi, Stephen
Wacker, and Scott Beatty.

Discover more at
www.dk.com

Contents

DK READERS

PROFICIENT
4
READERS

JLA AQUAMAN'S GUIDE TO THE OCEANS

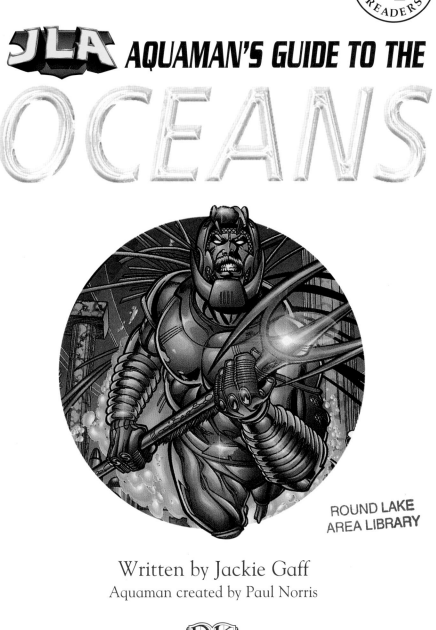

ROUND LAKE
AREA LIBRARY

Written by Jackie Gaff

Aquaman created by Paul Norris

Maiden voyage
Aquaman got his very own comic in February 1962.

Founder
The Justice League of America (JLA) was formed to battle aliens from the planet Appellax. Aquaman was a founder, along with the Flash, Black Canary, Green Lantern, and the Martian Manhunter.

Awesome oceans

Strap on your diving gear and get ready to leave the surface world and travel with me, Aquaman, on an extraordinary journey through my watery kingdom.

We have five oceans to explore— the Pacific, the Atlantic, the Indian, the Southern, and the Arctic. All five oceans flow into one another, making up one gigantic body of water.

ATLANTIC OCEAN

PACIFIC OCEAN

This water is salty, of course, unlike the fresh water of lakes and rivers. Each ocean contains smaller bodies of salty water called seas, bays, or gulfs.

Together, the oceans cover more than 70 percent of Earth's surface and contain nearly 98 percent of all its water! We have a long way to go and we'll have to move fast.

Are you ready? Then let's take the plunge!

The largest ocean is the Pacific. It is bigger than the other four put together, and large enough to swallow all the continents.

ARCTIC OCEAN

PACIFIC OCEAN

INDIAN OCEAN

SOUTHERN OCEAN

Sinking feeling
The city of Poseidonis sank beneath the waves 40,000 years ago, blasted into the depths after a meteorite hit the Earth.

Royal capital
Aquaman's underwater kingdom is called Atlantis. His capital city of Poseidonis lies on the floor of the Atlantic Ocean, protected by a vast crystal dome.

Hidden depths

If you could pull a huge plug and drain the oceans of all their water, you would be able to see broad, flat plains, high mountain ranges, and deep, narrow trenches—the hidden landscape of the ocean floor.

Trenches are the deepest parts of the ocean. The deepest is the Mariana Trench in the Pacific, which is almost 7 miles (more than 11 kilometers) below the water's surface. It could swallow the world's highest mountain, 29,028-foot (8,848-meter) Mount Everest, and still leave its peak 1 mile (1.6 kilometers) below the surface!

There are three main parts to the ocean floor—the continental shelf, which surrounds the land, the continental slope, and the deep ocean floor.

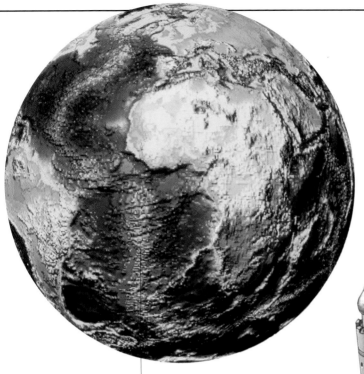

Mountain ranges called mid-ocean ridges run for thousands of miles through the Pacific, Atlantic, and Indian oceans. In places, the ridges peak into mountains that rise above the water to form islands.

Mid-Atlantic Ridge

The continental shelf slopes away from the coast to a depth of about 650 feet (200 meters). It ends at the continental slope—a cliff that drops to the ocean floor, over 2 miles (3 kilometers) deep.

The flattest areas of the deep ocean floor are called the abyssal plains—abyssal means "deep" or "bottomless." The abyssal plains are dotted with underwater volcanoes called seamounts.

Home sweet home
At the heart of Poseidonis is Aquaman's palace—his family home, as well as the seat of the Atlantean government.

7

Exploring underwater

Like other land animals, humans cannot survive without breathing air. They have to take an air supply with them when they want to explore the oceans. Scuba divers carry their air supply in tanks on their backs—"scuba" is short for "self-contained underwater breathing apparatus." Even with scuba gear, few people dive deeper than 100 feet (30 meters).

But underwater explorers have another problem. The deeper they dive, the more the water above them presses down on their bodies. At the bottom of the ocean, the pressure would flatten them into a pancake! A small submarine called a submersible with a very strong hull, or body, is designed to cope with the high pressure found deep beneath the water's surface.

Breathing space
Aquaman can breathe on land as well as underwater—unlike most Atlanteans, who can't survive out of the ocean.

Some submersibles are robots called ROVs (short for "remotely operated vehicles") while others can carry a small crew. Few submersibles can dive deeper than 3,300 feet (1,000 meters).

Bathyscaphes are crewed submersibles that can dive the deepest, and the record-holder is the *Trieste*. On January 23, 1960, it carried Jacques Piccard and Donald Walsh to the bottom of the Mariana Trench.

Air supply
To fight crime underwater, Batman has a rebreather in his Utility Belt. This gives him a few minutes of oxygen.

This submersible, the Atlantis Deep Explorer, *has room inside for three people. It collected objects from the wreck of the* Titanic, *at a depth of about 12,500 feet (3,800 meters).*

Mind over matter
Aquaman's greatest power is his ability to communicate telepathically (mind-to-mind) with ocean animals.

Home guard
Aquaman is the sworn protector of all sea creatures.

The living oceans

From sandy seashores to deepest depths, the oceans are home to thousands of animal species. Plants have a harder time in the sea because they need sunlight to survive, and the deeper you go in the ocean, the darker it gets. Plants can only live in shallow, sunlit water around the coasts or close to the ocean's surface.

Most ocean plants are so small that they can only be seen under a microscope. They are called phytoplankton, and they are the main food for swarms of tiny animals called zooplankton. Small fish feast on zooplankton, and they, in turn, are eaten by bigger fish, which are eaten by still larger animals. A system like this, in which creatures are dependent on one another for food, is called a food chain.

However, a few of the largest ocean creatures feed directly on zooplankton.

These include the blue whale, the biggest animal that has ever lived. Blue whales can grow to 100 feet (30 meters) long, and they can be heavier than 25 elephants. Despite this, they only eat zooplankton called krill, which are about the size of a human finger.

It takes a lot of krill to satisfy a blue whale—one whale can swallow as many as 30 million krill in a day!

Royal ride
Aquaman sometimes hitches a ride on the back of an enormous blue whale.

Blue whales do not have teeth. Instead, their mouths are lined with baleen plates—huge, hanging bristles that work like a giant sieve, filtering krill from vast mouthfuls of seawater.

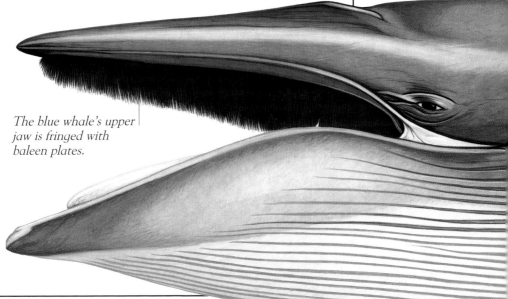

The blue whale's upper jaw is fringed with baleen plates.

Cursed
The baby Aquaman was cast out of his home because his blond hair was believed to be the mark of the Curse of Kordax.

Kordax
Born with scaly skin and blond hair, Kordax fought many battles with the Atlanteans.

Wonderful whales

The blue whale is not the only record-holder in the whale family. The sperm whale has the largest brain that has ever existed and is one of the ocean's deepest divers—it can dive down more than 1,600 feet (1,000 meters)!

Whales are found in every ocean around the world, from the steamy tropics to the icy poles. The whale family includes dolphins and porpoises, and scientists divide it into two main groups, according to the animals' feeding habits. Baleen whales, like the blue whale, sieve their food from the water. Other members of the baleen group are the fin whale, the gray whale, the right whale, and the humpback whale.

Members of the second whale group have teeth instead of baleen plates. They are called toothed whales, and they include sperm whales and dolphins.

With their fins and sleek bodies, whales look a little like fish. They aren't fish, though, but mammals, like humans. Like us humans, they need to breathe air, and they do so through blowholes on their heads. Toothed whales have just one blowhole, while baleen whales have two blowholes.

Dolphin mother
Fortunately, the baby Aquaman was rescued and raised by the dolphin Porm. She cared for him so well that he came to love her as a mother.

Aqua-boy
Aquaman's birthname was Orin. When he was ten, Orin briefly lived with lighthouse-keeper Arthur Curry. Luckily, Curry realized that Orin could not survive on land forever, and he urged the boy to return to the ocean.

For hundreds of years, the sea has inspired artists such as Japan's Katsushika Hokusai.

Ocean in motion

The oceans are never still. Waves continuously roll across the surface, currents flow like giant rivers, and water levels rise and fall every day.

The daily rise and fall of the oceans are called the tides. They are caused by the gravity of the Moon and the Sun tugging on the Earth. Water levels rise at high tide, and fall at low tide, and each day there are one or two high tides and one or two low tides.

Most waves are created by wind blowing across the water's surface, but vast waves called tsunamis are triggered by underwater earthquakes or volcanic eruptions. A tsunami is small out in the open ocean, but by the time it reaches the coast it will have grown into a gigantic wall of water.

These enormous waves can be more than 100 feet (30 meters) high. Tsunamis can cause terrible damage, killing people and wrecking buildings.

The world's major surface currents are also caused mainly by the wind. They help to shape the Earth's climate by moving large masses of warm or cold water around. For instance, the Gulf Stream carries warm water from the Gulf of Mexico toward the North Atlantic Ocean, where it warms the shores of Western Europe.

Substitute father
Curry and Orin became as close as father and son, and Aquaman later called himself Arthur "Orin" Curry.

Waves can be anything from gentle ripples to the huge breakers that surfers use to catch the ride of a lifetime.

Fame at last
Orin was 25
when he helped
the Flash defeat
a villain and
the surface
world first
learned of
Aquaman's
powers.

Royal surprise
When Orin
returned to
Poseidonis, he
learned that his
mother had
been queen of
Atlantis—
making him the
rightful king!

Shaping the coastline

As waves pound and crash against the coast, they eat into the land and wear it away. The seawater carries sand and pebbles that grind against the rock like sandpaper, wearing away weaker areas and shaping the coastline. In areas with soft rock such as limestone, waves may eat out sandy bays. In areas with hard rock such as granite, they may carve steep cliffs and headlands.

Sea caves begin as tiny cracks in steep, rocky cliffs. Over time, waves batter these cracks into holes, which gradually get larger and larger. Many sea caves are only big enough to hold one or two people, but some are enormous. The world's longest sea cave is Painted Cave on Santa Cruz Island off the coast of California.

With a length of nearly 1,320 feet (402 meters), it has room to park a row of 40 buses!

When caves form in a headland, they sometimes grow large enough to break through to the other side of the cliff and form an arch. If the roof of the arch then collapses, it leaves a pillar of rock called a stack jutting up from the ocean.

Queen
Soon after his coronation, Aquaman married Mera, an underwater queen from another dimension.

Pounding seas attack the coastline, carving out cliffs, caves, and bays.

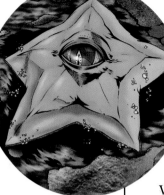

Deadly starfish
When an alien power invaded the Earth from outer space, the JLA dubbed it "Starro" because it looked like a starfish.

Starro could control people—even a hero like Batman—by sticking probes to their faces.

Living on the edge

Life is not easy for the animals that live along the seashore. Not only do they have to cope with a battering from the waves, but they are also in danger of being left high and dry when the sea retreats at low tide.

Most of the creatures that live on rocky shores have special ways of holding on to firm ground so that they are not washed away by the waves. Mussels produce sticky threads that glue them in place, while limpets use suction to clamp their bodies to the rock. Starfish are suckers, too—they cling using thousands of tiny tubes beneath their arms.

It is harder for animals to get a grip on the loose surface of sandy shores, and fewer kinds of creatures are found there.

Animals such as clams, crabs, and worms shelter from the crashing waves by digging holes deep into the sand on a beach.

When the water drains away at low tide, creatures with hard shells have the best chances of survival. Crabs and snails crawl into damp cracks in the rocks, while barnacles and limpets clamp their shells tightly shut until the sea returns.

Bottled menace
Aquaman helped fight off two attacks by Starro before the JLA imprisoned the deadly starfish in a fishbowl!

When the tide drops on a rocky shoreline, small pools of seawater are left in hollows. These are tide pools, and they often shelter animals such as fish, starfish, and sea anemones.

Charybdis
Aquaman lost his left hand when it was eaten by piranhas, driven to attack by Charybdis.

Handy replacement
Afterward, Aquaman wore an artificial hand, made of liquid metal that could change into a harpoon.

Tough nuts

Crabs belong to a group of animals called crustaceans, along with lobsters and shrimp. Unlike fish and mammals, crustaceans do not have bones. Instead, their soft bodies and jointed legs are covered and protected by a hard outer shell called an exoskeleton. There are thousands of species of crustaceans, and most of them live in the oceans.

With that many crustaceans, it is no surprise that they come in all shapes and sizes. Among the smallest are water fleas, which can sit on a pinhead, but the biggest can measure 13 feet (4 meters) across its outstretched legs. This monster crustacean is called the giant spider crab and is found in the seas off the coast of Japan. It looks like a spider, with a small body and long legs.

All crabs, some lobsters, and a few shrimp have clawlike pincers on their front legs, which they use to catch food. The most unusual claws belong to the male fiddler crab—one is much bigger than the other, and almost as wide as its body. This crab waves its nasty nipper to attract females or warn off other males.

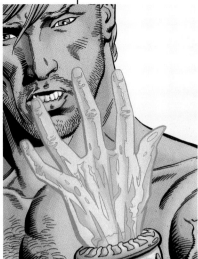

Graceful gift
The Lady of the Lake, caretaker of the Secret Sea, has given Aquaman a new hand made of magical water. With it, he can see visions, fight magic, and heal the sick.

Unlike other crabs, hermit crabs do not grow their own shell. Instead, they live inside the empty shell of a sea snail. When the hermit crab gets too big for its borrowed shell, it scuttles out to find a new, bigger one.

Underwater forests

Seaweeds are another coastal life form with a special way of beating a battering from the waves—they get a grip with a rootlike anchor called a holdfast. A seaweed's holdfast is not a true root, though, because unlike plant roots, it does not take in water and food. Seaweeds are not plants, in fact, but belong to a group of simple life forms called algae.

Most kinds of seaweeds grow near rocky coasts, where their holdfasts can latch on to a solid surface. They can be green, red, or brown, and the longest is the Pacific giant kelp, which grows to 200 feet (60 meters) – higher than a 20-story building!

Giant kelp forms vast underwater forests off western North America.

Aqua-farming
Kelp is farmed in special underwater greenhouses just outside Poseidonis. This seaweed is one of Aquaman's favorite foods.

Monster weed
This creature of the deep was composed of seaweed. It was also immune to Aquaman's telepathic powers.

These forests are home to thousands of creatures—half a square mile (1.3 square kilometers) of kelp forest can contain 80,000 animals! Kelp creatures range from tiny sea snails to crabs, fish, and even mammals such as the sea otter. They are also home to the world's largest slug, the California sea hare. This creature grows to a length of nearly 3 feet (90 centimeters).

Humans have also found all sorts of uses for seaweed, including eating it and using it to make everything from lipstick to ice cream.

The sea otter lives in the kelp forests of the Pacific. It wraps itself in kelp fronds and lies on its back to smash shellfish open with a stone—a rare case of an animal using a tool.

Walking salad
Aquaman used his telepathic control to summon up a cloud of hungry fish to chase off the monster.

Aquaman's ally
Although Aquaman has many enemies, he is supported by a group of firm friends. His closest ally is Tempest.

Water wife
Tempest's wife Dolphin was born to land-dwelling parents. She was stolen from them as a baby and learned to survive underwater.

Colorful coral

Some of the ocean's most colorful creatures live in and around coral reefs, from blue-lipped giant clams to neon-striped angelfish. A coral reef is a limestone outcrop that forms in the warm, shallow coastal waters of tropical regions. The world's largest is the Great Barrier Reef off the northeastern coast of Australia. This massive structure stretches for over 1,250 miles (2,010 kilometers). Amazingly, this enormous ocean landmark was built by tiny coral animals that measure less than 1 inch (2.5 centimeters) in length.

A single coral animal is called a polyp, but polyps rarely live alone. They prefer to stay together in groups called colonies, which can be made up of thousands or even millions of individuals.

Coral polyps have jellylike bodies, and most kinds make a hard limestone skeleton. When they die, the skeletons are left behind, and over the years, these build up into a structure that we call a coral reef.

The hundreds of kinds of coral form differently shaped structures. Some look like bundles of stiff spaghetti, others are like loose-leaved cabbages, and the brain coral looks like a human brain!

Coral prison
At one point, Tempest was held captive in a prison made from sharp coral.

One of the most colorful creatures in a coral reef is the orange clownfish.

The Shark
A sworn enemy of Aquaman, the Shark is desperate to win control of Poseidonis.

Shark defense
Riding on their trusty shark mounts, the Atlantean Guard forms the first line of defense for the underwater kingdom.

Shark attack

Another creature that likes coastal waters is the oceans' most famous hunter, the great white shark. With teeth as sharp and as jagged as steak knives, this shark is certainly designed to kill. But despite its fearsome reputation, the great white rarely attacks humans. Instead, it prefers to prey on seals.

Sharks are fish, and the largest, the whale shark, is also the biggest kind of fish. It grows to about 40 feet (12 meters) in length, longer than a bus. However, like the other ocean giant, the blue whale, it mainly feeds on zooplankton.

The smallest sharks, such as pygmy sharks, rarely get longer than 10 inches (25 centimeters). Different species of sharks are found in every ocean.

Great white sharks
grow to over
20 feet (6 meters),
as long as two cars.
They can open their
mouths as wide as
3 feet (1 meter)
before taking a bite
out of their prey!

Some hunt for prey, while
others sit and wait. The Port
Jackson shark, for instance, lies on
the sea floor of shallow coastal
waters around Australia and New
Zealand. It eats other seabed
creatures, such as sea urchins and
crabs, shoveling them up with
its downward-pointing
mouth and
crunching them
to pieces in its
powerful jaws.

Narrow miss
Although he is
the sworn
protector of all
sea creatures,
Aquaman has
had a few close
calls with
sharks.

Undercover operation

For many ocean creatures, life is a very serious game of hide-and-seek—hiding from enemies that are seeking out their next meal! Some animals try to stay out of trouble by blending into the background. This cunning tactic is called camouflage.

Two of the oceans' most expert hiders are brilliant at blending in with seaweed. Their patterned skin makes sargassum fish and weedy sea dragons very difficult to spot as they float among weeds. The weedy sea dragon is a kind of sea horse, and sea horses are actually fish!

Some spider crabs are called decorator crabs because of their ability to disguise themselves.

Martian shape-shifter
When it comes to camouflage, no one can beat another JLA member, J'onn J'onzz, the Martian Manhunter. The last survivor of a Martian race, J'onn J'onzz can shape his body into any form he wants.

They stick anything they can find, from seaweed to scraps of wood, onto their shells to camouflage themselves from predators.

Other ocean creatures use camouflage to help them catch their prey. The tasseled wobbegong shark's patterned skin lets the creature blend perfectly with the sand and rocks on the seabed. The shark lies in wait on the ocean floor, waiting to ambush an unsuspecting fish.

At 18 inches (45 centimeters) long, the weedy sea dragon is one of the largest kinds of sea horses.

Rule bending
Another JLA shape-shifter is the amazing Plastic Man. He can stretch or squash his body into every shape under the Sun—animal, vegetable, or mineral!

Deadly defenses

Be warned—some ocean animals are armed with a poisonous bite or sting. They are more likely to attack an enemy than hide from it, and a few of them can be deadly to humans who stumble across them. The blue-ringed octopus is not much bigger than your hand, for instance, but it packs a poisonous punch that can kill an adult human in minutes. This deadly creature lives in coral reefs in the Pacific and Indian Oceans.

Another potential killer is the Australian box jellyfish, or sea wasp. The slightest touch of this jellyfish's long tentacles produces incredibly painful whiplash marks on human skin. In the past, it was common for badly stung people to die, but nowadays there is an antidote that helps most victims to recover.

Deadly enemy
One of Aquaman's deadliest foes is Black Manta, the villain who was responsible for the death of Aquaman's son.

Evil exchange
Black Manta traded his soul to change from a human into a hideous sea creature.

The stonefish is not only deadly, it is also a master of disguise—it looks just like a rock when it hides on the floor of its coral-reef home. Its deadly defenses are the sharp, poison-packed spines on its back. These contain enough venom to kill a human—so make sure you don't step on one!

Thirsty work
The Thirst is one of Aquaman's most gruesome enemies. Anyone touched by this monster is instantly turned into a mindless zombie.

The stonefish is one of the most poisonous sea creatures.

The jet set

Unlike the blue-ringed octopus, most other octopuses and their relatives, squid, are gentle creatures. Their first line of defense is camouflage, since they can quickly change the color and pattern of their skin to blend in with their surroundings. If things get really serious, they opt for a quick getaway, jetting backward by sucking in seawater and pumping it out through a funnel on the side of their body. They may also pump out a cloud of inky liquid to hide their escape.

These ocean jet-setters have boneless, baglike bodies ringed by tentacles—octopuses have eight tentacles, while squid have ten.

Fast swimmer
Aquaman's superpowers make him the speediest mover in the ocean.

Squid head
With the body of a squid instead of a head, Cap'n Squid can blast Aquaman with a high-power jet of ink.

The giant squid is one of the ocean's most mysterious creatures. None have ever been caught alive, but dead ones washed up on beaches can be over 50 feet (15 meters) long—no wonder sailors once told tales about ships being sunk by them!

These tentacles are lined with powerful suckers that are used to catch and hold prey. Octopuses and squid prey on fish, crustaceans, and shellfish. Hidden beneath their baggy bodies are beaklike jaws that are powerful enough to crunch through shells and fish bones.

The smallest octopuses measure about 1 inch (2.5 centimeters) from tentacle tip to tentacle tip. However, the largest, the giant Pacific octopus, can measure 16 feet (5 meters) across!

Eight-legged friend
Aquaman has an octopus ally known as Topo. This eight-legged giant has helped our hero on more than one occasion.

Wandering ways

Sea turtles are famous for their long-distance journeys. Thousands of green turtles, for instance, spend most of their lives feeding off the coast of Brazil. But when it is time for them to breed, they swim as far as 1,500 miles (2,400 kilometers) out into the Atlantic Ocean, heading for the tiny island of Ascension. After they arrive, the females dig nests in the beach sand and lay their eggs. When they are finished, it is time for the long journey home!

Regular round trips like these are called migrations, and they are usually made by animals looking for the best places to feed or breed. Blue whales are serious travelers. They spend the summer feeding in the Arctic Ocean or the seas around Antarctica.

Landlovers
Unlike most citizens of Poseidonis, who are happy to stay in their home under the sea, the Landlovers explore the world above the waves. These travelers include the whale-man Blubber, the mermaid Sheeva, and Lagoon Boy.

When winter comes, they head for warmer waters near the equator to give birth.

European eels migrate across the Atlantic Ocean to lay their eggs in the Sargasso Sea, an area of water near Bermuda. The journey is so long that the eels die afterward from exhaustion.

Sheeva
Blubber and Lagoon Boy first met Sheeva at a birthday party for King Orin. Their first trip to the surface nearly ended in disaster as Blubber was injured by frightened New Yorkers.

Female green turtles lay their eggs in nests on beaches during the night. They do not hang around to bring up their babies, though. When the baby green turtles hatch, they are on their own and have to fend for themselves.

Cold friends
After he left Arthur Curry, Aquaman spent some time in the chilly Arctic. Here, he befriended a group of Inuit.

During his time with the Inuit, Aquaman became very close to a girl named Kako.

Icy oceans

It is no wonder that blue whales head for the equator in winter— the Arctic and Antarctic are the world's coldest places year-round! But although the water in these polar regions is icy, it is still packed with life. Small polar animals include krill, crabs, starfish, and sea spiders. Larger animals range from sharks and other fish to seals, penguins, and whales.

When it comes to keeping warm, seals, penguins, and whales all have extra help. Beneath their skin, these animals have a thick layer of fat called blubber. This works like a combined winter coat and pantry, storing heat and food energy.

Seals are very much at home in the water. Although they are mammals, like us humans, and need to breathe air, they are also superb swimmers and excellent divers.

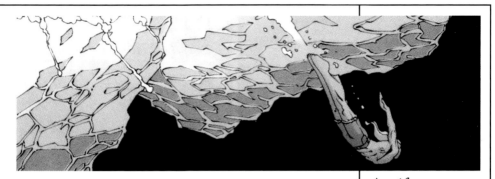

They have sleek, torpedo-shaped bodies and very powerful flippers. The diving champion is the elephant seal—it can swim as deep as 5,000 feet (1,500 meters) and stay underwater for an hour! The most ferocious seal is the leopard seal. It hunts everything from fish and penguins to other seals.

Antifreeze
Even the chill of a polar sea does not stop Aquaman from swimming. His powers allow him to dive into any stretch of water, from the equator to the poles.

Whales make their homes in oceans all around the world—even in the freezing polar seas.

Polar bears are such good swimmers that they are often found swimming several miles from land or ice.

Polar peril
During his time spent in the frozen north, Aquaman came face to face with a vicious polar bear. After a fierce battle, the underwater hero triumphed, but only with the help of Kako.

Polar animals

Penguins and polar bears never meet—this is because polar bears are only found in the Arctic, while penguins only live in the seas and oceans south of the equator.

Although polar bears spend most of their time on land, their favorite food is seals and they will quickly plunge into the water when they are hunting. Paddling with its massive front legs, a polar bear can speed along at 6 mph (10 km/h).

Penguins are even faster, with a top underwater speed of over 20 mph (30 km/h). These birds are at their best when in the water. Unlike most other birds, they cannot fly through the air and can only waddle around on land. If they want to move quickly on land, they lie on their bellies and toboggan across the slippery ice.

Some penguins can also make spectacular leaps. One champion high jumper is the Adélie penguin, which lives in the icy wastes of the Antarctic. It is only about 2 feet (60 centimeters) tall, but when it wants to get out of the water, it can leap more than three times its own height up on to the ice.

Partners in crime
The Penguin was a member of the original Injustice Gang, a group of super-criminals funded by arch-villain Lex Luthor. Their aim? To destroy the Justice League of America!

Mother emperor penguins spend the winter out at sea, feeding and getting fat. The fathers are left behind on land, keeping the eggs warm by balancing them on their feet.

Hidden depths
Noble is the ruler of an ancient city that lies in the deepest part of the ocean. Here he rules a mysterious race of creatures called Lurkers.

The warrior king Noble and his race of Lurkers use bioluminescence to light their way through the ocean.

Living in the dark

Even in the clearest of ocean waters, sunlight can only reach a depth of 3,300 feet (1,000 meters). Below this, no light can penetrate, and the water is inky black all the time. This is the dark zone, and it is home to some of the spookiest creatures in the ocean.

The biggest problem for animals that live in the dark is finding a meal. Because there's so little light, eyes are not much use, so some animals rely on body cells or antennae that are sensitive to the tiniest movement. The hairy angler, for instance, has so many antennae that it looks more like a porcupine than a fish.

Most deep-ocean creatures deal with the darkness by making their own light. This ability to glow in the dark is called bioluminescence, and it is often used to attract prey.

The deep-ocean anglerfish, for instance, has a wandlike fin just above its mouth. The tip of this fin glows with an eerie blue light. Any creature that is attracted to the glowing light is snapped up by the anglerfish's massive mouth and its long, viciously sharp teeth.

Dragonfish are even more scary. Their bait is 6.5 feet (2 meters) long, while the fish itself measures just 6 inches (15 centimeters) long.

Depth of evil
The evil sorcerer Hagen wages war on Aquaman from his headquarters in the ocean depths. He uses his dark arts to magically change ocean creatures into nightmarish monsters.

The deep-ocean anglerfish lures prey with the glowing light that dangles above its gaping mouth. This fish may be no longer than a human hand, but its huge, stretchy stomach means it can gulp down prey twice its own size!

Ocean harvest

The oceans are a rich resource, supplying us with everything from food to precious gems. Every year, millions of tons of fish are harvested from the oceans, and around the world millions of people rely on fishing for their food and their jobs. Seaweed is another healthy ocean food, while much of the salt we use in cooking comes from seawater.

The soft, squashy skeletons of animals called sea sponges are gathered from sandy seabeds for use as natural bath sponges. Some of the colorful creatures that live in coral reefs are even more useful, because they produce powerful chemicals that can fight illnesses such as cancer. Scientists create new, highly effective medicines by copying the chemicals produced by these animals.

Warring for wealth
Driven by a powerful desire to control the riches of the deep, Ocean Master fought to overthrow Aquaman and take his place as the king of Atlantis.

Some ocean products are harvested more for their beauty than for their usefulness. The ancient Romans used murex sea snails to make a purple dye, which they valued more highly than gold. The shell of the abalone, a type of sea snail, is so beautiful that it is used to make jewelry. Most precious of all, though, are the pearls that grow inside some oysters.

UHN!

Battling brothers
This fight to the death was between Ocean Master and Aquaman, who were both fathered by the wizard Atlan.

Pearls form if a tiny piece of grit gets inside an oyster's shell. Layers of a substance called nacre are laid over the grit to smooth it and stop it from scratching.

Oceans of energy

Where would people be without fuel for cars, trains, and planes? How would we manage without electricity to power equipment, and to light homes and workplaces? Most transportation fuels are made from oil, while most electricity is generated by burning oil and gas in power stations. Large reservoirs, or stores, of this useful oil and gas energy are hidden in rocks beneath the ocean floor. They are tapped by drilling down to them from offshore platforms.

But oil and gas also cause problems. When they are burned, they release the gas carbon dioxide into the air, where it works like a blanket, trapping the Sun's heat.

Clean machine
Solar energy from the Sun is another clean power source. It is what the JLA uses to power the Watchtower, their base on the Moon.

Many scientists think that this buildup of carbon dioxide is making Earth's climate warmer. They call the temperature rise "global warming."

Fortunately, the oceans are also a source of clean, renewable energy. Tidal power stations use the tides, for instance. Water is trapped behind a barrier at high tide. At low tide, the water flows through turbines to produce electricity.

Force field
When he is racing around, JLA speedster the Flash is powered and protected by an energy known as the Speed Force.

Offshore oil and gas platforms are huge structures where workers live while they drill for fuel. Some platforms have extremely long legs that rest on the ocean floor, while others float on shorter, air-filled legs. The oil and gas are either piped back to land or carried by tanker ships.

45

Oceans in danger

Humans are harming the oceans and the creatures that live beneath the waves. Good fishing grounds have been ruined by taking too many fish too quickly. This overfishing means that there is not enough time for new generations of fish to be born, grow into adults, and have babies of their own. If numbers continue to fall, some kinds of fish may disappear.

Pollution is another danger to the oceans. When sewage and garbage are dumped offshore, they poison the water and the animals that live in it. Even beach litter can kill—an animal can choke to death if it swallows a plastic bag.

Defender of the deep
Aquaman has pledged his life to protecting his underwater kingdom and its creatures from harm.

Toxic avenger
Another superbeing who is devoted to protecting the environment is Swamp Thing.

Hundreds of animals may be killed when an oil tanker runs aground and spills its load. Local communities also suffer if the oil spill pollutes fishing grounds and tourist beaches.

The good news is that humans are trying to clean up their act. Not only are scientists coming up with high-tech ways of dealing with oil spills, but many governments have passed laws stopping overfishing and banning garbage-dumping in the ocean. Every person on the planet can play their part in protecting the oceans, by taking litter home and treating all ocean creatures with respect.

Kingfish
The evil Kingfish used poisons given off by Gindola fish under his command to control the citizens of Poseidonis and turn them against Aquaman.

Every year, hundreds of tons of garbage and debris are washed up onto our beaches and coastlines, creating an eyesore for us and a hazard for wildlife.

Glossary

Algae
Life forms that range in size from a tiny single cell to seaweeds 200 feet (60 meters) long. Most algae live in water.

Antarctic
The region of the world around the South Pole. This cold part of the world has a large landmass that is covered year-round in thick ice sheets.

Arctic
The region of the world around the North Pole. Although there is no landmass in the Arctic, the area is covered with a thick sheet of ice. This ice sheet gets bigger and smaller as the seasons change.

Baleen plates
The large, fringed plates that hang inside some whales' mouths. The whales use them to sieve tiny animals from seawater to eat.

Bioluminescence
The ability of a plant or animal to create light. Many sea creatures use these lights as bait to attract prey.

Camouflage
The ability to hide against a background by using a matching pattern and/or shape.

Crustaceans
Boneless animals with a hard outer shell that supports and protects their bodies, such as crabs and lobsters.

Equator
An imaginary circle drawn around the Earth at its widest part that is the same distance between the North and South Poles.

Global warming
The gradual increase in temperatures around the world. Most of this increase has been blamed on human activity, such as burning fossil fuels (oil, coal, and gas) and pollution.

Headland
A narrow piece of land that sticks out into the sea.

Ocean currents
The movement of large masses of water around the oceans.

Overfishing
Taking too many fish out of the sea, and not leaving enough fish to reproduce and replace those caught.

Phytoplankton
Microscopic plants that make up the start of the food chain in the oceans.

Renewable energy
Also known as alternative energy, this is a form of energy taken from a natural and nonpolluting source, such as the wind and tides.

Reservoirs
Huge stores of a resource, such as oil or water.

Scuba
Short for "self-contained underwater breathing apparatus," consisting of tanks containing air, which divers strap to their backs to breathe underwater.

Tsunami
An enormous wave caused by an earthquake or volcanic eruption.

Turbines
Wheels with blades that spin when water or air passes over them.

Zooplankton
Microscopic animals (crustaceans and fish) that provide food for much larger creatures, such as whales.

Index